Flowers

Illustrated by Rene Mettler
Created by Gallimard Jeunesse,
Claude Delafosse and Rene Mettler

MOONLIGHT PUBLISHING/FIRST DISCOVERY

A crocus
pushes out of the bare land.
It is spring.

Crocus flowers
may be purple,
white or yellow.

A tall orange pistil (1)
is hidden inside
each flower.

Can you also see
the stamens (2)
dusted with pollen?

Insects are attracted by the scent
and colour of the flowers.
They settle on them and drink their nectar.

Pollen from the stamens brushes
onto their legs, and is carried
to the pistils of other flowers.

This is a dandelion, from flower-bud to seed.

First it is a bud, then the flower spreads open its petals.
An insect, passing by, leaves pollen on the pistils.

The flower fade
and the fruit form

they fly off on their tiny parachutes!

As the seeds ripen,

Strawberries flower and ripen in the same way.

First come
the buds, then
the open flowers.

The petals wither and
drop. The fruit
grows until
it is ripe...
and ready for
us to eat.

All fruits come from flowers.

Apple

Aubergine

Bean and
aubergine flowers
have fruit too:
they are vegetables.

Bean

Sometimes, the flowers are better to eat than the fruit.

Saffron comes from the dried pistils of the wild saffron crocus.

Cloves are the dried flower buds of the clove tree.

Globe artichokes are the buds of the artichoke flower.

Camomile
and lime-flowers
make delicious,
sweet-smelling teas.

Capers are buds
from the caper shrub.

Sunflowers and rape
flood the fields with yellow.

Their seeds are crushed
to make oil.

Sunflowers turn their faces
to follow the sun
as it moves across the sky.

Sage

Orchid

Daffodil

Foxglove

Sweet violet

Clover

You can learn
to recognise flowers
by their different
shapes, colours
and scents.

Harebell

Iris

Florists sell these cultivated flowers
at their stalls and in their shops.

These flowers are related
to flowers that grow in the wild.

Daisy

Lily

Can you
match up the
cultivated
flowers to
the wild ones
named here?

Viola

Eglantine

Pink

Buttercup
Ranunculus acer

Press some common
flowers between sheets
of blotting paper,
under a weight.
When they are dry,
stick them carefully
onto paper.

Pressing
flowers

Rare flowers like these mountain ones
are protected by law,
and we must not pick them.

Edelweiss

Gentian

Enjoy flowers where they grow,
in meadows and gardens and parks,
and only pick them
if you know it is allowed.

FIRST DISCOVERY – pioneering the exciting technique of the double-sided printed overlay.
More titles are available:

ABOUT ANIMALS
THE EGG
BIRDS
FARM ANIMALS
THE ELEPHANT
WHALES
THE HORSE
MONKEYS & APES
BEARS
CATS
THE MOUSE
THE LADYBIRD
THE BEE
DINOSAURS

ABOUT PEOPLE
COLOURS
UP & DOWN
LIGHT
PICTURES

MUSIC
HOMES
THE CASTLE
FLYING
ON WHEELS
BOATS
HANDS, FEET AND PAWS
BABIES

ABOUT NATURE
FLOWERS
FRUIT
VEGETABLES
THE TREE
WATER
THE RIVERBANK
UNDER THE GROUND
THE JUNGLE
EARTH AND SKY
THE SEASHORE
WEATHER

Translator: Sarah Matthews
Editorial adviser: Alastair Martin

ISBN 1 85103 144 8
© 1991 by Editions Gallimard
© British edition 1992 by Moonlight Publishing Ltd
First published in the United Kingdom 1992
by Moonlight Publishing Ltd, 36 Stratford Road, London W8
Printed in Italy by Editoriale Libraria